j581

Rahn, Joan Elma, 1929–
    Grocery store botany. Illustrated by Ginny Linville
Winter. [1st ed.] New York, Atheneum, 1974.
    54 p. illus. 22 cm.
      SUMMARY: Describes the anatomy of some common food plants
and gives directions for twenty-five simple demonstrations and experiments illustrating the functions of some plant parts, especially
those used for food.

      1. Botany—Experiments—Juvenile literature. 2. Plants, Edible—
Juvenile literature. [1. Botany—Experiments. 2. Plants, Edible]
I. Winter, Ginny Linville, illus. II. Title.

QK52.6.A33 1974   581'.028
ISBN 0–689–30435–6 (lib. bdg.)   74–75567
                                    MARC

74 [4]   AC

GROCERY STORE BOTANY

Joan Elma Rahn

GROCERY STORE BOTANY

ILLUSTRATED BY

Ginny Linville Winter

Atheneum · 1974 · New York

To Timothy Owen

Contents

GROCERY STORE BOTANY

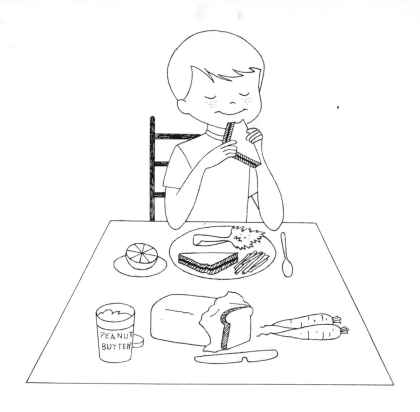

Introduction

Suppose for lunch you had an orange, a peanut butter sandwich, some carrot strips, and a celery stalk. You know the names of these foods, but do you know what they really are? Where they come from? What we eat when we eat them?

An orange is the fruit of a tree. The flour that made the bread in the sandwich comes from some small, dry fruits; they are the kernels of wheat plants. Peanut butter is made from peanuts, which are seeds. Carrots are roots. Did you know that celery stalks are parts of leaves and not stems?

Everything in this meal came from plants. All of our food comes from living things—some from plants and some from animals, but mostly from plants.

Flowering plants give us most of our food. There are many kinds of flowering plants, and all, at some time in their lives, produce flowers. At least they do if they live long enough. We usually eat carrots before it is time for the plants to bloom. The little bean sprouts in Chinese food are young mung bean plants only a few days old. If they had been allowed to become several weeks old, they would have had flowers.

All flowering plants have roots, stems, and leaves. If they live long enough to have flowers, then they also can bear seeds and fruits. From some plants we eat roots, and from some others stems or leaves. We eat very few flowers but many kinds of seeds and fruits.

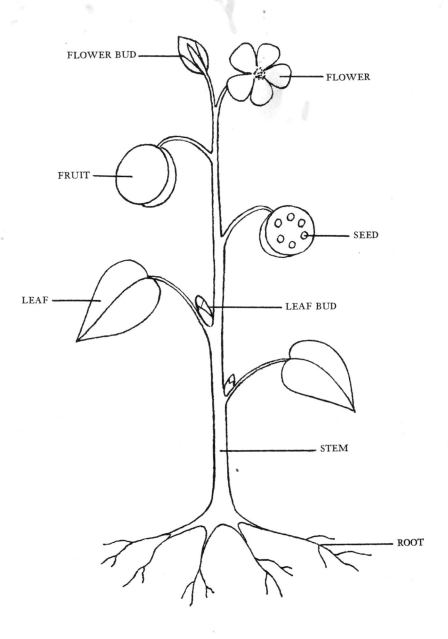

FLOWER BUD

FLOWER

FRUIT

SEED

LEAF

LEAF BUD

STEM

ROOT

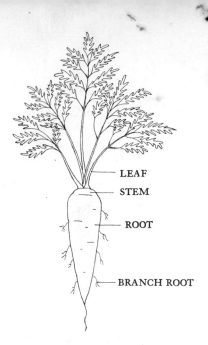

LEAF

STEM

ROOT

BRANCH ROOT

Roots

Most roots grow in the ground. Here they absorb water from the soil and anchor the plant firmly. Some roots, like carrots and sweet potatoes, become very thick, for they store a great deal of food, especially sugar or starch. So we pull them up and eat them. If you grow your own carrots in a garden, or if your store sells them with the tops on, you can see an entire plant with root, stem, and leaves. The stem is the very small greenish portion at the top of the root. The leaves grow from the top of the stem.

If the carrot has not been cleaned well, you may also see small branch roots. The branch roots have smaller branch roots, and these may have even finer roots. You cannot see all of them, however, because most of them broke off and remained behind when the carrot was pulled from the soil. The more its roots branch, the more firmly a plant is anchored in the soil.

SOMETHING TO DO — I
The smallest roots absorb water from the soil. In each branch root and in the main root is a vein that carries both water and food. You can stain part of the vein easily with colored water. Dilute some red food coloring with about the same quantity of water. Mix them well by stirring. Cut off a carrot about a half-inch from the bottom and throw the small piece away (or eat it). Put the carrot, cut side down, in the colored water.

Wait an hour or two, then remove the carrot and rinse it

in plain water to wash off any food coloring clinging to it. Now cut across the carrot about a half-inch above the first cut. The center of the carrot will be stained red. This part of the vein is called the *xylem*; it carries water upward toward the stem.

The other part of the vein is the *phloem*; it carries food both upward and downward. The colored water does not stain the phloem, so it is somewhat harder to see than the xylem. In a carrot root, the phloem appears as a light orange ring around the xylem.

Put the carrot back in the colored water and wait for several hours (overnight, if you like). Then cut the carrot in half the long way. See if you can follow the veins all the way from the root through the stem and into the leaves (or just into the bases of the leaves, if they have been removed).

The green leaves of a plant make its food. The phloem carries the food down to the root, which stores it until some other part needs it. Then the phloem carries the food upward to that part.

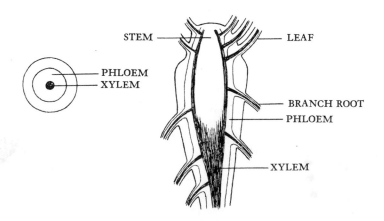

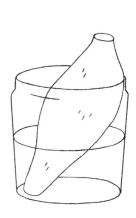

You can watch how a plant uses the food in a root. Get a sweet potato and put it in a jar with some water. The end with the large scar should be up, and the end with the small scar should be down.

Watch the sweet potato for several weeks. It will sprout stems, leaves, and more roots. It uses its food as it forms these new parts. Be sure to add water to the jar from time to time to keep the plant from getting dry. If you keep the plant in sunshine, it will grow into an attractive vine. In sunshine, leaves form new food that a plant uses as it grows.

How many other kinds of roots do you eat? Beets, parsnips, turnips, and rutabagas all store much food, and we eat these thick roots as vegetables.

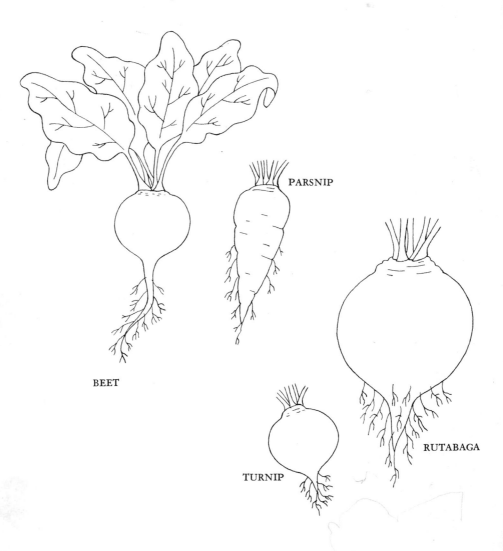

PARSNIP

BEET

TURNIP

RUTABAGA

CASSAVA PLANT   GINGER PLANT

One dessert we get from a root is tapioca. It is prepared from the root of the cassava plant, which grows only in warm climates. The root of the ginger plant gives us the spice we use in gingerbread. Licorice for candies comes from the roots of the licorice plant.

Did you ever wonder how root beer got its name? Its flavor comes from the bark of the roots of the sassafras tree.

BRANCH OF SASSAFRAS TREE

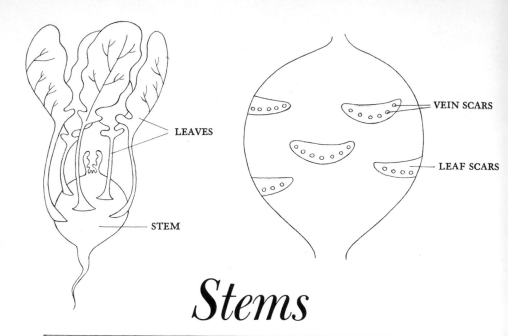

LEAVES

VEIN SCARS

LEAF SCARS

STEM

Stems

Most stems grow above ground. Leaves grow out from them, and sometimes flowers and fruits do, too. Most of the stems we eat are vegetables.

SOMETHING TO DO — 3

A kohlrabi is a large, swollen stem. Like other stems, it has leaves. If you pull the leaves off, you can see leaf scars on the stem. Look closely at a leaf scar, and you will see several dots in it. When you took the leaf off, you broke the veins that ran from the stem into the leaf. The dots mark the locations of the broken veins.

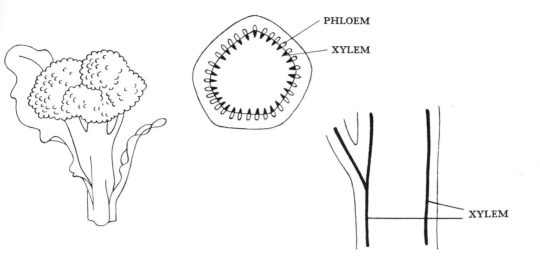

PHLOEM

XYLEM

XYLEM

SOMETHING TO DO—4

The next time your mother buys fresh broccoli, ask her for a stalk. Cut a little bit from the lower end to get a clean, fresh surface. Examine the cut end. You should be able to see a ring of many small veins. Each vein has both phloem and xylem in it. You can stain the xylem in the veins as you did the xylem in the carrot. When the red color appears at the top of the stalk (in a few hours), cut a little more from the lower end to get another fresh surface.

In each vein the xylem will be red. The phloem will not be stained and will appear green. Each strand of phloem lies a little closer to the outside of the stem than does the xylem. Use a magnifying glass if you have one. It will help you to see this more clearly.

Now cut the stem the long way so that you also cut through at least one leaf. You can see the veins running up and down the stem. Perhaps you can see a vein that branches off from the vein in the stem and goes into a leaf. If not, your cut probably went between two veins in the leaf. Just make another cut parallel to your first one and very close to it. If you still cannot see the connection between the veins in the stem and leaf, make more cuts through this leaf or start on another one.

Find the small green flower buds at the top of the broccoli stalk. Make some cuts across the little stems that hold these buds to see if the veins run into them.

SOMETHING TO DO — 5

Asparagus stems have small, pointed leaves. Pull off some of the leaves near the bottom of an asparagus stem, and you will find a very small bud just above each leaf scar. You probably can see the leaves in the bud, but its stem may be too short to see clearly.

Now remove a leaf about halfway up the main stem. You may find that its bud has grown into a short branch about a quarter of an inch long with its own small leaves. Still higher on the main stem, you may even see branches large enough that they have small buds under their own leaves.

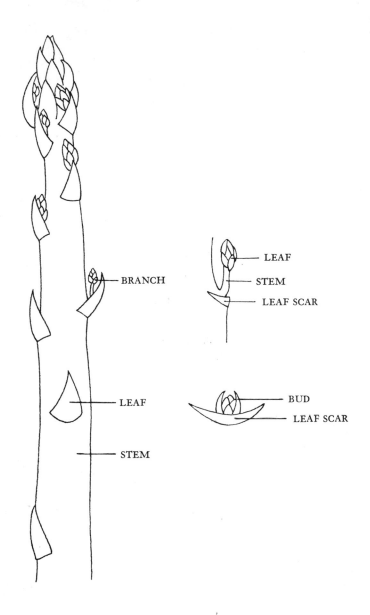

BRANCH

LEAF

STEM

LEAF

STEM

LEAF SCAR

BUD

LEAF SCAR

You might like to stain the veins of an asparagus stem. Can you find any difference in the arrangement of the veins in asparagus and broccoli stems? Cut the stem the long way to see if the veins in the main stem connect with those in the buds.

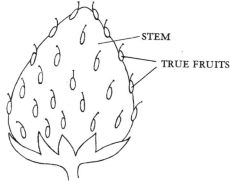

STEM

TRUE FRUITS

STRAWBERRY

PISTIL

STAMEN

SEPAL

PETAL

STRAWBERRY FLOWER

SOMETHING TO DO—6

Strawberries are not really berries at all. The strawberry flower grows on a tiny green stem that sticks up into the flower. The flower produces the real fruits of the strawberry plant. These are the little yellow flecks that sometimes get stuck between your teeth. While the flower produces these fruits, the little green stem grows into a strawberry. A ripe strawberry is really a red stem, but it is so delicious that we usually call strawberries fruits and eat them as we eat fruits.

The next time you eat a fresh strawberry, cut it open exactly down the center. Do you see the white veins that go from the stem to the little yellow fruits?

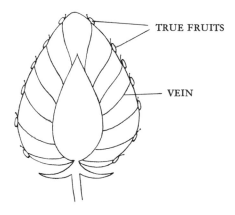

TRUE FRUITS

VEIN

You probably guessed by now that veins run through all the parts of a flowering plant: from root to stem and from stem to leaves—and to flowers, fruits, and seeds, too, when the plant has them.

Not all stems grow above the ground. *Tubers* are thick underground stems, and they store much food, especially starch. White potatoes are tubers, even though some persons think of them as roots. Tubers have buds and leaves. The buds of white potatoes are called "eyes." You can find them in depressions on the surface of the potato. The leaves of the tuber are very small. Usually they fall off long before the potatoes reach the store, so you cannot see them. Perhaps you can find the leaf scar below each bud.

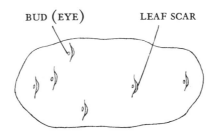

BUD (EYE)   LEAF SCAR

SOMETHING TO DO — 7

If you keep a white potato in a little water in a large shallow dish (like a pie plate) and keep it in sunshine, you can watch horizontal stems called *rhizomes* sprouting from the potato. Later, tubers will form from the tips of the rhizomes. Other stems will grow upright; when a potato is planted underground, these stems grow up into the air. They bear the green leaves of the plant. Roots grow from the stems.

RHIZOME
TUBER
ROOT

One of our favorite spices, cinnamon, comes from the bark of the stem of the cinnamon tree. The sticks of cinnamon that you may use to stir your hot cocoa are curled pieces of bark.

Leaves

Leaves make nearly all the food that plants need to grow and reproduce. Other green parts of plants make the rest of the food.

The process by which plants make food is called *photosynthesis*. *Photo* means light, and *synthesis* means a putting together of different things and a making of something new. So photosynthesis means a making of something—food—in light. Most stems hold their leaves in the air where they receive the sunshine they need for photosynthesis. Leaves that do not receive light, like leaves on underground stems, do not make food.

The next time you eat spinach for dinner, notice its dark green color. Most leaves have a green pigment called *chlorophyll*. This pigment is as necessary for photosynthesis as light is. Most leaves are green and photosynthetic. Leaves without chlorophyll, like the pale leaves inside a cabbage, do not produce food. Green stems, like those of broccoli, make some food, but generally leaves produce most of it.

In photosynthesis, leaves produce sugar. Then the plant changes the sugar into other kinds of food, like starch, fats, proteins, and vitamins. We need all of these things in our meals.

Leaves are important to us because photosynthesis makes all the food we eat. Everything we eat comes from either a plant, an animal that ate plants, or an animal that ate animals that ate plants. No matter what we eat, the food first was made by plants, and most of it was made by the leaves of flowering plants.

Even though they manufacture so much food, most leaves do not have a great deal of food in them, for the phloem carries it away. Some of it goes to roots or tubers, which store it. Some goes to growing parts of the plant that use it right away —like stem tips, root tips, and new leaves. Some goes to fruits and seeds. However, leaves are rich in vitamins, and so they make good vegetables or salad greens.

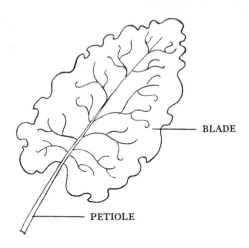

BLADE

PETIOLE

Most leaves have two parts: the *blade* and the *petiole*. If your mother buys fresh spinach or beet tops, you can easily see them both.

The blade usually is flat, though in some leaves, like those of spinach, it may be a little crinkly. The petiole is the stalk of the leaf; it looks something like a stem and can easily be mistaken for one.

Spinach leaves and beet tops are called *simple,* for the blade consists of just one piece. Do you remember the feathery appearance of the leaf of a carrot plant? Its blade is divided into many small parts. Such leaves are *compound*.

In some cases, we eat the petioles and not the blades of leaves. The blades of rhubarb leaves are poisonous, but the big, thick, red petioles make good desserts when cooked. Although the blades of celery leaves are nutritious, most persons prefer the thick, crispy petioles. Supermarkets usually chop the tops off celery before they sell it, but if you look in the center of a bunch of celery, you can find small leaves with their blades. Is a celery leaf simple or compound?

Some leaves have no petioles, but consist only of a blade. Cabbage and lettuce leaves are examples.

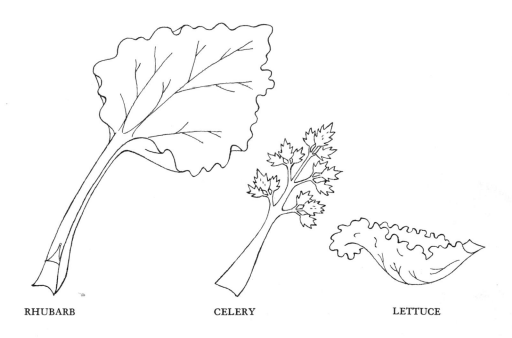

RHUBARB   CELERY   LETTUCE

You might like to examine the vein patterns in leaves. There are two main types: *netted* and *parallel*.

Spinach, beet tops, Swiss chard, cabbage, lettuce, and celery all have netted vein patterns. The main vein branches into smaller veins, and these branch into smaller and smaller veins. Some of the small veins meet making a network throughout the blade. In most leaves, such as those of lettuce or cabbage, this is quite clear, but if the veins in your leaf are hard to see, hold it up to the light and look through it. A magnifying

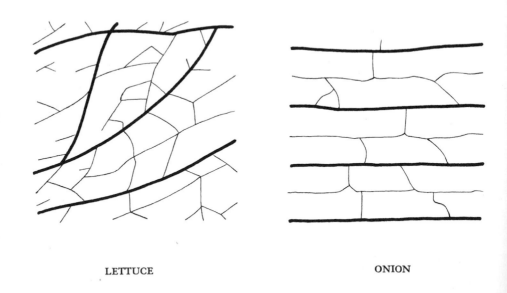

LETTUCE   ONION

glass will help, too. You also might like to put the cut end of the leaf in colored water to stain the veins.

Take one of the thin, dry, papery leaves from the outside of an onion and hold it up to the light. The onion has a parallel vein pattern. Most of the veins run parallel to each other. If you look closely, however, you will see a few short veins that connect the parallel ones.

All leaves grow from stems. Some, like the leaves on broccoli and asparagus stems, grow at well separated places on the stem. In some other plants, the leaves grow so close to each other that they form a head, like that of lettuce or cabbage. Such heads really are large buds.

A bud consists of a very short stem from which grow either leaves, flowers, or both. A bud with leaves is a leaf bud, one with flowers is a flower bud, and one with both is a mixed bud. Some buds contain smaller buds; these grow from the stem, one at the base of each leaf except for a few of the youngest leaves. Some buds are surrounded by bud scales, which are modified leaves. The heads of cabbage and lettuce and the smaller heads of Brussels sprouts lack bud scales.

SOMETHING TO DO — 10

If you cut a head of cabbage in half from top to bottom, you will see the leaves growing from the stem in the center of the head. Pull some of the leaves off, one at a time. Above each

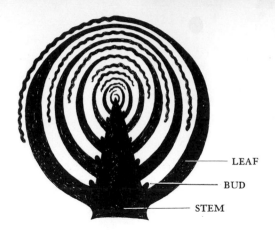

LEAF

BUD

STEM

leaf scar, you will find a small bud.

The outermost leaves are the oldest ones. The youngest leaves grow from the tip of the stem near the center of the bud.

A bunch of celery is really a large bud, too. It has leaves and buds growing from a stem, although the shapes of these parts differ from those of cabbage.

SOMETHING TO DO—II

An onion bulb is another large bud. Bulbs store food, and so the leaves of onion bulbs contain more food than many other kinds of leaves. The thin, papery leaves toward the outside are bud scales.

If you cut across the bulb, the way onions are cut to put on hamburgers, its thick, white leaves will look like rings, one inside the other. As in other buds, the oldest leaves are toward the outside, and the youngest toward the inside.

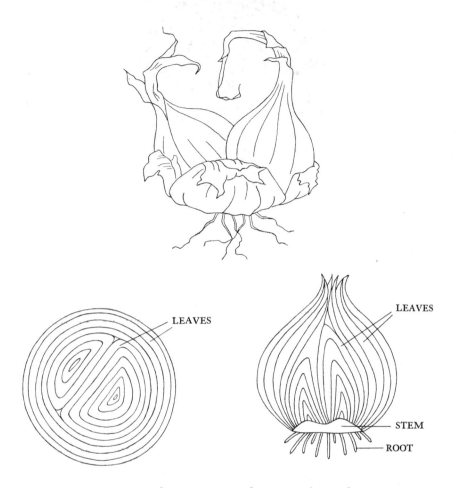

You may see more than one set of rings; this is because one of the small buds on the stem has grown into a larger bud. This is really a bulb within a bulb. We can also call this growing bud a young branch. If you plant an onion, each of its buds may grow into a new onion.

If you cut an onion bulb the long way, you will see that its leaves grow from a very short stem as they do in a head of cabbage. If your cut goes exactly down the center of one of the growing buds, you will see that it has its own small stem and that its stem grows from the main stem of the bulb. There probably are some small, dry roots at the bottom of the stem.

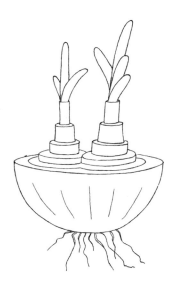

SOMETHING TO DO—12

Get a jar with an opening small enough to support an onion. Fill the jar with water almost to the top. Place the onion, root end down, on the jar. Watch the onion for several days. When several roots have appeared, cut across the middle of the onion and discard the upper half. Watch it for several more days. Which grow faster—the youngest or the oldest leaves?

Some other leaves we eat as vegetables or salad greens are dandelion leaves, endive, chicory, Chinese cabbage, kale, and collards.

Cooks use some leaves to give interesting flavors to their recipes. Rosemary leaves or the ground leaves of sage, thyme, or marjoram improve the taste of chicken. Pizza owes some of its flavor to oregano leaves. Perhaps your mother adds a bay leaf to some of her stews or roasts. Parsley goes well with many foods, and watercress makes a pungent addition to a green salad.

The flavors of spearmint chewing gum and peppermint candies come from the leaves of spearmint and peppermint plants.

One of our common beverages is made from leaves. We brew tea from the leaves of the tea shrub.

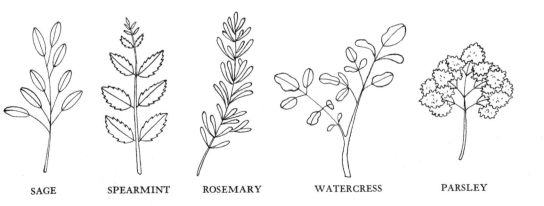

SAGE   SPEARMINT   ROSEMARY   WATERCRESS   PARSLEY

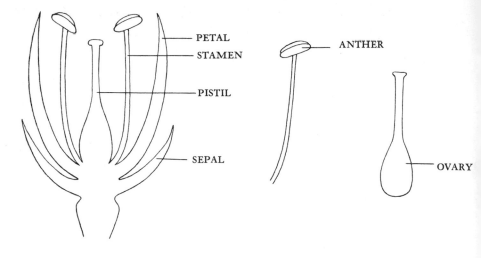

Flowers

Our meals include very few flowers, and those we do eat usually are still in the bud stage and are very small. It is difficult to see their parts clearly. Before looking at one of these flowers, you might want to learn the parts from the drawing. Most flowers have four kinds of parts: sepals, petals, stamens, and pistils.

Sepals usually are green and look a little like leaves. Before the flower opens, the sepals are on the outside and easy to see, for they usually cover the other flower parts. When the flower opens, the sepals may be partially hidden by the petals.

Petals come in various colors and combinations of colors but usually are not green. They lie a little closer to the center of the flower than the sepals do.

Even closer to the center are the *stamens*. At the top of each stamen is a sac called an *anther*. It produces the *pollen* of the plant.

In the center of the flower is the *pistil* or sometimes several pistils. If pollen lands on the pistil, the bottom part of the pistil, called the *ovary*, usually grows into a fruit with one or more seeds in it.

The numbers of these parts are different in different kinds of flowers. Some of the most common numbers are: 3, 4, or 5 sepals; 3, 4, or 5 petals; from 3 to 10 stamens; and 1 pistil. Sometimes there are 20 or 30 or even more of some of these flower parts. Sometimes some of them are missing completely.

SOMETHING TO DO — 13

Examine one of the flower buds at the top of a broccoli stalk. Choose the largest bud. Can you find the 4 sepals, 4 petals, 6 stamens, and 1 pistil? The green sepals enclose the other flower parts. The petals are almost transparent in most of the buds, but you may find yellow petals in buds ready to open.

If your mother will allow it, keep the broccoli stalk in

water for several days, and the buds may open and show their yellow petals. Broccoli smells bad after a few days in a warm room, so try to keep it as fresh as possible. Every day give it clean water and cut a little off the bottom of the stem. In warm weather, it would be a good idea to keep it outside.

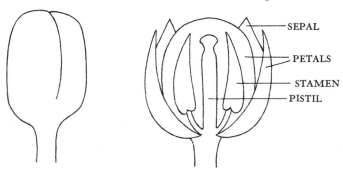

Cloves are dried flower buds. Used whole or ground up, they add a spicy flavor to foods as different as ham and cookies. Because we store them dry, cloves can be very brittle. Drying also makes all of the flower parts brown. If you want to examine them, soak a few cloves in water overnight to soften them. Four short, stiff sepals point upward or outward, and four petals enclose the many stamens and the single pistil.

The crinkly surface of cauliflower consists of many flower buds that just barely began to form and then stopped. They do not develop into flowers.

Flowers are not important to us as foods, but they are very important because of the fruits and seeds they produce. Without them, our diets would be very poor indeed.

Fruits

You have probably eaten several kinds of fruits today—maybe even more than one kind at each meal, for fruits provide us with most of our food. Some, like peaches or oranges, we all recognize as fruits. Others we call vegetables or cereals, and many people do not know they are fruits.

SOMETHING TO DO—14

Can you find at least a dozen fruits or foods made in part from fruits in this menu? If you can't now, you should be able to after you finish this chapter.

Breakfast
> Orange juice
> Cornflakes with bananas and milk

Lunch
> Spaghetti with meat balls and tomato sauce
> Dill pickle
> Cantaloupe

Dinner
> Steak with salt and pepper
> Rice
> Green beans
> Salad of avocado on lettuce
> Cherry pie

Every kind of fruit forms from a pistil in a flower and contains one or more seeds. If the fruit is soft and juicy, and if its seeds are small, we may eat the entire fruit—seeds and all.

SOMETHING TO DO—15

Try to get a tomato with the stem still attached to it. One of the small cherry tomatoes will do. Can you see any evidence that it once was part of a flower? While the pistil of the tomato flower was developing into the fruit, the petals and stamens fell off; but the sepals remained. If no one removed the stem, the five green sepals should still be there, too. (Large tomatoes may have more than five sepals.)

Cut the tomato across the middle to find the seeds. A thin wall divides a small tomato into two sections called *carpels*. On either side, the wall swells into a *placenta* that supports the seeds. (Large tomatoes have three, four, or even more carpels, each with its own seeds.)

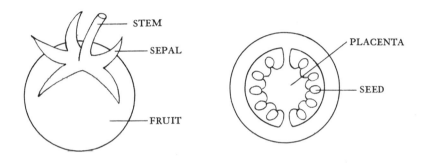

Some fruits have parts too tough, too hard, or just not tasty enough to eat. You may not like the fuzzy skin of a peach, but you can eat it. Most of the rest of the fruit is juicy and delicious, but the pit in the center is hard and stony. It may even be too hard to crack open with a nutcracker, but someday you will find a peach with a cracked pit; inside it you will see one seed. Peach seeds are slightly poisonous. Eating just one probably would not harm you, but several of them could make you sick.

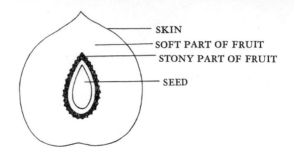

SKIN
SOFT PART OF FRUIT
STONY PART OF FRUIT
SEED

Apricots, plums, cherries, and olives resemble peaches in having stony pits with one seed inside. Did you know that prunes are dried plums?

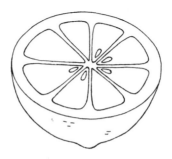

SOMETHING TO DO—16

Cut across a lemon to see how many carpels it has. The pistil of the lemon flower from which this fruit came had the same number of carpels. Most carpels have one or two seeds.

When you have the chance, compare an orange, grapefruit, tangerine, or lime with the lemon. All of these are citrus fruits.

SOMETHING TO DO—17

Cut across a cantaloupe as indicated by the drawing. Notice the hard outer rind and the three groups of seeds. Cut across

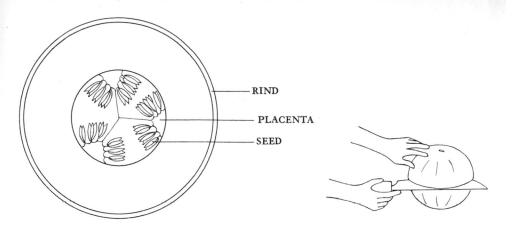

RIND

PLACENTA

SEED

a cucumber (or a pickle, which is just a young cucumber preserved in salt or vinegar). Compare the cucumber with the cantaloupe. We usually call a cucumber a vegetable, but it is also a fruit, for it contains seeds, and it ripened from an ovary.

Be sure to look at the inside of your next Halloween pumpkin when you hollow it out. Notice how much it resembles the cantaloupe. It is a fruit, too.

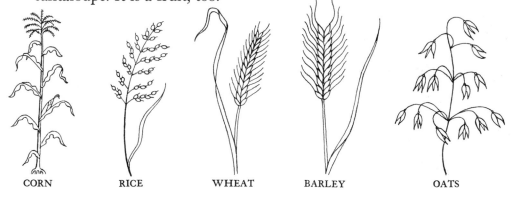

CORN   RICE   WHEAT   BARLEY   OATS

A few fruits look more like seeds than fruits. This is especially true of the kernels of cereals like corn, rice, wheat, oats,

CORN   RICE   WHEAT   BARLEY   OATS

CORNFLAKES   PUFFED RICE   PUFFED WHEAT

BREAD   MUFFIN   COOKIES   PIE

NOODLES   MACARONI

and barley. Each kernel consists almost entirely of a single seed. The outer part of the fruit is so thin and sticks to the seed so well that you can hardly tell where the fruit ends and the seed begins.

Although the kernels of cereals look small and insignificant, they contain much starch, and starch is our main food source of energy. You probably start your day with one of the cereals listed above. If you don't eat cold cereal or oatmeal, then you may have pancakes, waffles, or toast, all of which were made from flour. Most kinds of flour are the starch removed from cereal kernels. Have you ever watched your mother use flour to make bread, muffins, cookies, cakes, or pie crust? Noodles, spaghetti, and macaroni are made from flour, too.

Whenever you have the opportunity, examine any of the following to convince yourself that they really are fruits:

blueberries

avocado

green beans (the whole pod)

watermelon

squash

dates

red or green peppers

okra

eggplant

persimmon

grapes

Examine any other food you may think is a fruit.

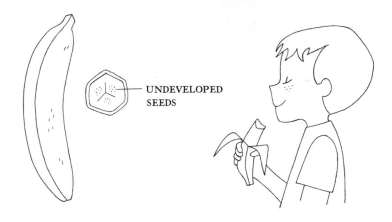

UNDEVELOPED
SEEDS

A few fruits, like navel oranges, bananas, pineapples, and some grapes, are seedless. This could cause you difficulty in determining if something is a fruit or not, but usually you can find some very small, poorly developed seeds. The tiny black dots in bananas, for instance, are seeds that just began to form and then grew no more.

Some fruits are more than just the product of a single pistil. Remember the strawberry, which is a stem with some tiny yellow fruits on its surface? Apples and pears are mostly stem, too. The stem surrounds the true fruit, which is just the center of the core.

SOMETHING TO DO—19

Get two apples. Examine both ends of one of them. Because of its weight, the apple hangs upside down on a tree. Therefore, the stem end is the real bottom of the apple. The opposite end, called the blossom end, is the true top. At the blossom end you should be able to find five small sepals around a little hole in the apple. A ring of many small, dry stamens extends out of this opening. The petals fell off long ago, but the sepals and stamens remain on the apple fruit.

Now cut one of the apples across the middle. Cut the other one from top to bottom, so that the knife goes through both the stem end and the blossom end. Compare what you see with the drawings.

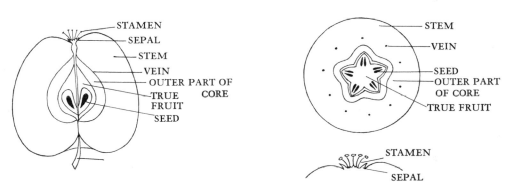

In a cross section, the five carpels of the fruit look like a star. Each carpel has two seeds. Can you find ten veins in the stem portion? These veins mark the edge of the core. Usually you eat only the stem. Unless you are very hungry, you don't eat the true fruit of the apple.

Some things we call fruits are not really single fruits, but several small fruits growing so close together that they resemble a single one.

SOMETHING TO DO—20

Break a raspberry (or a blackberry) apart to separate the individual fruits. Can you find one seed inside each fruit?

ONE FRUIT

A pineapple consists of many fruits surrounding a stem. The fruits are so close to each other that they become fused together, but you can tell where they are by observing the diamond pattern on the outside of the pineapple. One fruit lies just beneath each "diamond." Each fruit is attached to the stem in the center of the pineapple. In fact, it is mostly stem that we eat in a pineapple. We usually throw away the hard core in the center of the stem, but in a very ripe pineapple, even this may be edible.

We use a few fruits more for their ability to flavor other foods than for their own food value. The caraway "seeds" in rye bread and the dill "seeds" in a jar of pickles are really fruits. So, too, are anise "seeds" used to flavor cookies.

Black pepper is ground from small, dried berries called peppercorns. Real vanilla flavor comes from the dried fruits of the vanilla orchid.

DILL   ANISE   CARAWAY

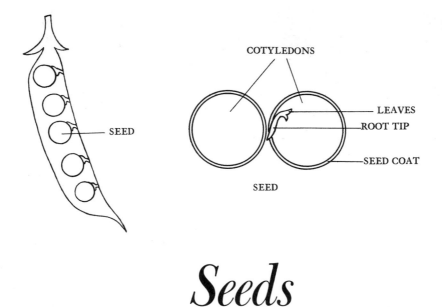

COTYLEDONS

LEAVES
ROOT TIP
SEED COAT

SEED

SEED

Seeds

Not all fruits are good to eat, but their seeds may be. Each seed contains a young plant called an *embryo*. The embryo needs food to keep it alive, and the seed stores food. For this reason, many seeds are nutritious for us, too.

SOMETHING TO DO — 21

When your mother buys fresh peas in the pod, ask her for one of the pods. Open it. By now, you should be able to tell that the pod is a fruit and that the peas in it are seeds.

A seed coat surrounds each seed. You can remove it easily.

Then the embryo is all that remains of the seed. Split the embryo into two halves. Each half is a thick leaf called a *cotyledon*. These leaves store most of the embryo's food. Attached to one of the cotyledons is the rest of the embryo. (It was attached to both cotyledons, but when you separated them, you broke off one cotyledon.) You probably can see two very tiny leaves and a root tip. Embryos usually do not begin to grow while seeds are still in their fruits, but if you shell a lot of pea pods, you may find a few seeds with roots growing out of them.

When a pea seed is planted, the root tip grows down into the soil. Between the leaves is a stem tip so small you probably cannot see it; but this stem tip will grow above the ground after the seed germinates. From it will come all the stems and leaves of the pea plant. Later, flowers will grow from the stems and produce more pea pods.

You might like to compare lima beans and kidney beans with a pea. All are seeds, and most of their food is in the cotyledons of the embryos. A peanut with its papery red covering is a seed, too.

SOMETHING TO DO—22

If you have difficulty seeing the attachment of cotyledons to the rest of the embryo of a pea or bean, you might be able

45

to see the attachment more clearly in a young avocado plant. It will take a few months to get a young seedling from a seed, however.

Remove the seed from an avocado fruit and place the seed wide end down in a wide-mouthed jar. Add enough water to make it about a half-inch to an inch deep. Add more water whenever necessary to keep it from drying out. Avocado embryos grow slowly, so it may be a month or even two or three before you see the root emerge. A few weeks later the stem will emerge.

As the stem grows thicker, it will push the cotyledons farther and farther apart. As the space widens, you should be able to see where the cotyledons are attached to the stem.

By now you have a young avocado tree. If you plant it in soil in a flowerpot, you will have a nice ornamental plant.

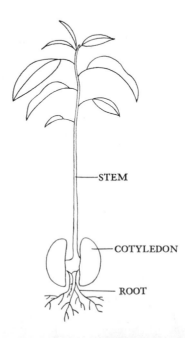

"Alike as peas in a pod." You probably have heard this expression. The peas in one pod usually do look very much alike, but this is not true of all seeds. No two individuals, whether plant or animal, are exactly alike. Sometimes the differences are hard to find; in other cases, they are so obvious it is difficult to find two individuals that look alike.

SOMETHING TO DO—23
Buy a package of pinto beans. A pattern of spots covers their seed coats. Can you find two identical pinto beans?

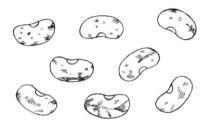

Most nuts are fruits, but usually we eat just their seeds—walnuts, pecans, hickory nuts, Brazil nuts, coconuts, pistachio nuts, and cashews.

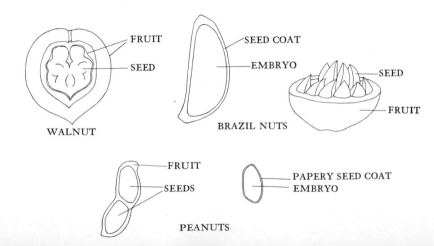

Several spices come from seeds—mustard, poppy seed, nutmeg, and mace. Mace tastes much like nutmeg and comes from the outer part of the nutmeg seed. This outer part is called an *aril*.

We use seeds to make several of our beverages. Chocolate comes from the seeds of the cacao tree, and we brew coffee from the "beans" of the coffee tree. The seeds of the cola tree are used in the making of cola drinks.

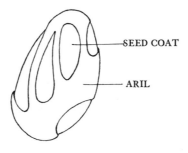

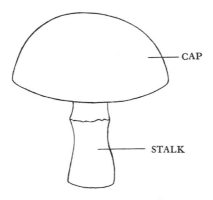

CAP

STALK

Plants Without Flowers

Not all plants produce flowers. We eat only a few kinds of these nonflowering plants. One kind is the mushroom.

SOMETHING TO DO—24
Examine a mushroom. Can you find flowers? Seeds? Fruits? Leaves? Stems? Roots? A mushroom has none of these parts. Its stalk, which looks a little like a stem, does not have veins inside it as stems do.

You can check this by cutting a little off the bottom of the stalk and placing the mushroom in colored water. If you cut the stalk open after an hour or so, you will see that the water does not rise in a special tissue; it moves throughout most of the stalk.

Mushrooms are *fungi*. Not only do fungi lack the parts typical of flowering plants, they also lack chlorophyll. For this reason mushrooms cannot make their own food. Instead, they live on the excrement of animals and the remains of dead or dying plants. By decaying these materials, mushrooms get their food.

One fungus, so small that you cannot see just a single plant without using a microscope, is yeast. Each plant consists of only one cell. Yeasts reproduce by forming new cells that grow out from the sides of the old cells and then separate from them. Like other fungi, yeasts cannot make their own food. In nature, they use the sugars in fruits as their food source.

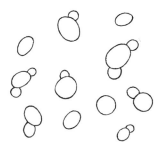

Dissolve a teaspoon of sugar in a quarter cup of lukewarm water. Add one package of bakers' yeast. This package contains millions of live yeast cells. Mix it well with the sugar and water. Watch this mixture every few minutes for about an hour.

In a little while the mixture will become bubbly. The process by which the sugar combines with other chemicals and growth and new cells are produced, releases a gas called carbon dioxide. This gas is what makes the bubbles.

When a baker adds yeast to bread dough, the bubbles of carbon dioxide cause the dough to rise. When the dough has risen as much as he wishes, he bakes it in an oven. After baking, the bubbles appear as holes in the bread.

Plants and Our Food

Vegetarians are persons who eat only plants. Though most persons are not vegetarians, many of the poor people throughout the world can afford very little meat or other animal products in their meals. Therefore, it is fortunate that plants can give us a balanced diet.

The nutrients we must eat to stay healthy are carbohydrates (starch and sugars), fats or oils, proteins, vitamins, and minerals.

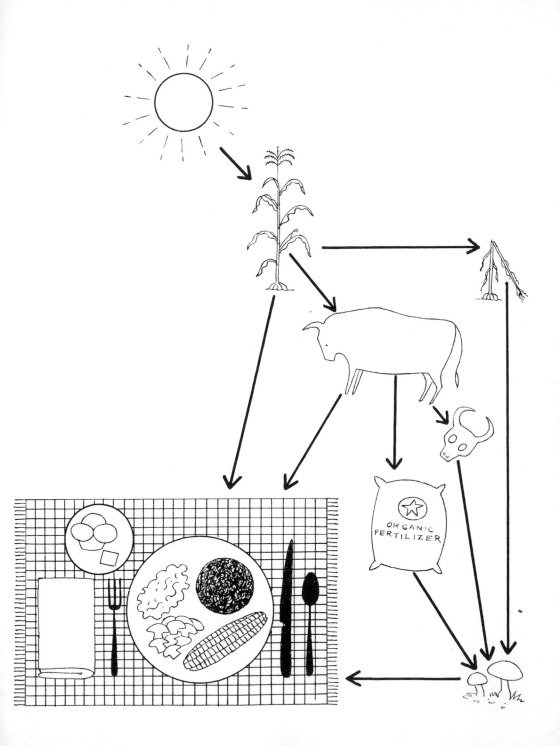

We get plenty of starch from cereals, bananas, and potatoes. We extract table sugar from the roots of sugar beets and the stems of sugarcane. Many common fruits are rich in sugar; when ripe, most of them have a sweet taste.

Some foods rich in oils are peanuts and other nuts, olives, and avocados. Oleomargarine is made from oils derived from several plant sources—corn kernels, soybeans, or safflower seeds.

Most plants do not contain much protein. Therefore vegetarians usually include in their diets the few plants that do: beans, peas, and whole-grain cereals. It is the outer part of cereal grains that is rich in protein; when the outer part is removed—as it is in making white flour—most of the protein is lost.

We get vitamins and minerals from many different kinds of fruits and vegetables.

Human beings are not the only eaters of plants. Animals eat them, too, and use their nutrients. The animals' bodies convert the plant nutrients into other kinds of nutrients, especially animal proteins.

Persons who can afford to do so usually get most of their protein by eating meat or some other animal products like milk, cheese, and eggs. These items also allow us to have greater variety in our diets, but we would not have them were it not for the plants that nourished the animals.